The Secret of Life...

P.D.Hodkin

Horizons New Publishing Ltd
42-44 Copthorne Road
Felbridge, RH19 2NS
United Kingdom

Website: www.horizonsnew.com

Illustrations by Susan Harrison
SOOZIHUMOR
www.susanharrison.biz

I don't know, but I've been told

That I will die when I grow old

And all that I have will then be lost

My family, friends and things that cost

Should I live my life as bold as can be?

Is what I leave what's left of me?

Or is there a future beyond the grave?

And should I work my soul to save?

If there is an answer to be found

Will I find it in the ground?

Perhaps I should open my eyes to look

There may be something in this book

CONTENTS

About the Author

Peter lives in Surrey with his wife Terrie.

By profession Peter has been a computer programmer and a lawyer, both disciplines requiring logic and systematic thinking.

Having been raised in two different religions - and having looked over a wide range of faiths – Peter has always been more interested in what religions share than in their differences.

In seeking to answer the really big questions of existence Peter has often pondered whether religion has anything to offer science, and vice versa. He concludes that they do. As Peter has written elsewhere, what all religions have in common is the belief that a person is not an object. This, he says, accords with science, since no living thing behaves like an object would. Arguably a body may be an object, but whatever animates it is not. Whatever "life" is, it does not simply respond to things according to the laws of science, but has a genuine power of choice. This is fortunate, because If we were all just objects, life would be meaningless, valueless and nothing would really matter. Only the fact that we have a power of choice, and are not just objects, gives life meaning and value. Only then does it matter how we treat one another. Science gives us knowledge, but religion gives us meaning.

While Peter writes his poems in a beautiful, light, breezy and fun filled fashion - you may just find yourself in them. He describes them as a voyage of self-discovery.

The Reunion

P.D. Hodkin

O happy day it is
When two old friends,
Having long been parted,
Are re-united.

And so it is when Science and Religion

Find themselves, once again,

travelling the same path.

"Yo," says Science, by way of

greeting,

"It seems an age since we last met."

"Yes," says Religion, with smile a-

beaming,

"Thomas Aquinas[1], sometime saint,

put us together,

And called me your big brother in

1267,

And we enjoyed each other's

company

---

[1] Saint Thomas Aquinas (1225 - 1275) Famous Italian philosopher and priest who described Christianity as a higher science.

For a goodly and godly while.”

“Aye,” says Science, in sad

reminiscence,

“But then we went, it seems, different

ways.”

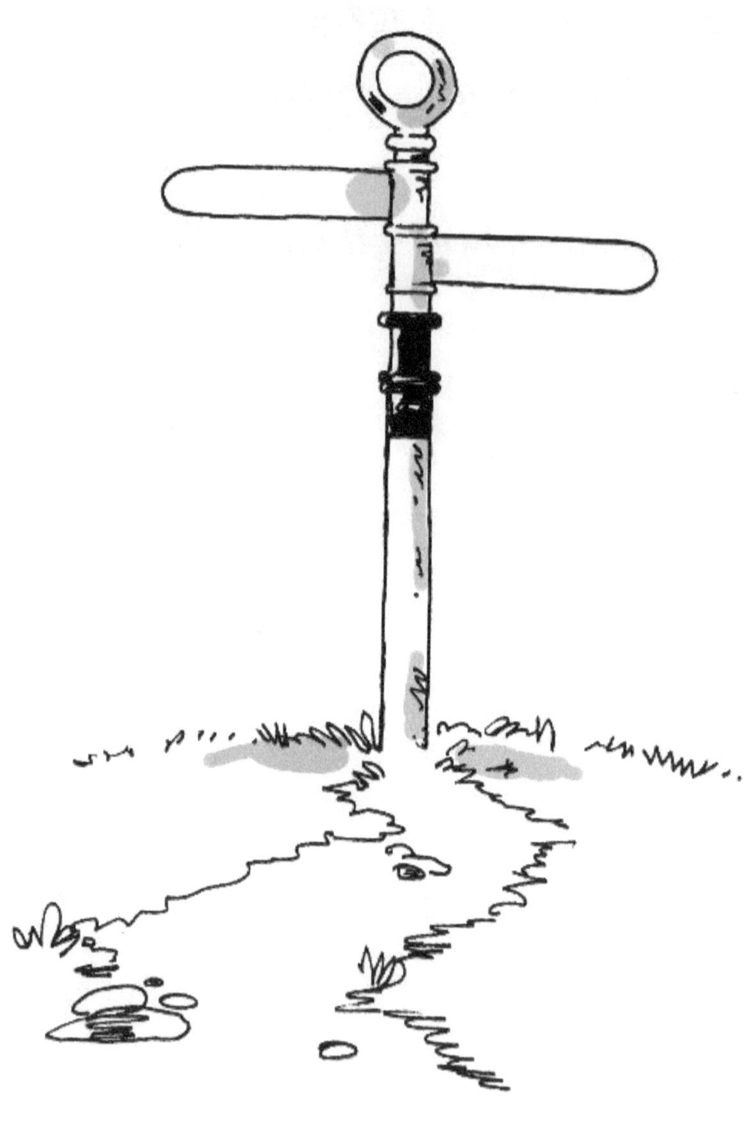

Each had thought they went off with Truth.

"But my Truth," says Religion, "had rested in Sacred Doctrine,
And, clothed in dogma, did not move with the times."

"Whilst my Truth," says Science, "had evolved and revealed,
Casting aside unnecessary vestments
And seemed to reside many miles from Sacred Doctrine."

"**Y**es," says Religion, "but recently
I started to strip my Truth
Of stories and myths. And lo, I
thought, our Truths naked
Could really be the same,
Just dressed differently for a while."

Looking about, Science says,
"Do you see my Truth sitting
there at my feet?"
"Yes," Religion replies, "and I see
mine also there.
Are two Truths really one?
Tell me Science, how did you get
here?"

" Since we last met, I have worked with Mathematics and

Observation

And brought precision and

understanding to the laws of nature.

My friend, Newton[2], defined forces

and motion

With simple formula.

And my friend Einstein[3] found the

greatest equation of all,

---

[2] Sir Isaac Newton (1642 - 1727) English mathematician and scientist who discovered the Laws of Motion.

[3] Albert Einstein (1879 - 1955) German born physicist who determined that all matter was really energy, and that the amount of energy locked in any particular piece of matter was equal to its weight (or mass) multiplied by the speed of light squared. Hence his famous formula: E=MC2 – where E is the energy in a piece of matter, M is its mass and C is the speed of light.

That the energy in any piece of
matter
Was equal to its mass times the speed
of light times the speed of light.
Which meant that even the smallest
piece of matter
Contained an awful lot of energy
And releasing just some of that
energy
Brought forth the Nuclear age.

e=mc²

But more than this, it transpired that matter

Was only seemingly of substance;

On close examination its atoms

consisted almost entirely of space

And the little apparently solid material

Was, in fact, just condensed energy.

Whatever energy was?

So the Universe, which seemed to consist

Of matter, energy and space,

In reality consists of only energy and

space.

The Universe is a vast cloud of
energy particles,
In an even greater space.

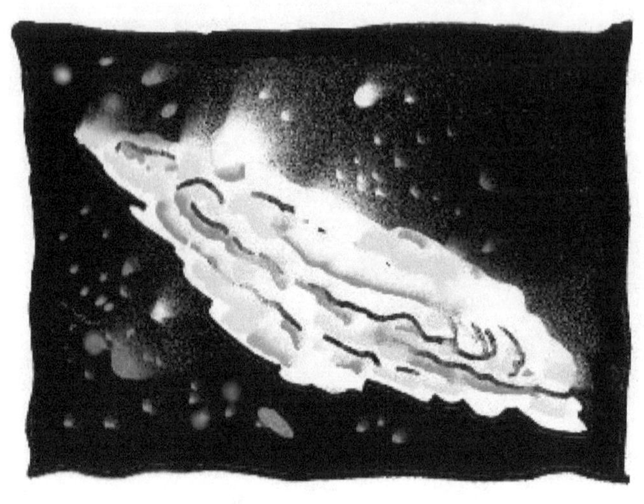

And when those energy
particles are densely
congregated
We have the things that seem solid
The stars and planets, and bodies of
all kinds.

And those energy particles have
the most amazing properties.
They simultaneously
Both attract, through gravity,
And repel, through impact and
emission,
Other energy particles.
Indeed exerting a force, both inward
and outward
On every other energy particle in the
Universe."

"That is very curious," says
    Religion,
"An energy that both pushes and
pulls?"
"Yes," says Science, "and what is
more, it seems
That if you add all of the pushing
energy in the Universe
And all of the pulling energy
They come to the same.
So that, on one view,
All of the energy in the Universe
Cancels itself out;
A net balance of energy of zero.
Thus we have a Universe of equal
and opposite

Making an apparent something out of nothing."

*"**I**f I may sum up what you are
saying," says Religion,*

*"Science has found a Universe
consisting*

Of a large cloud of energy particles

(sometimes called matter)

In a space.

With each energy particle

apparently having no substance,

But nonetheless affecting every other

energy particle there is;

The motion of one affecting the

motion of all."

"That is right," says Science, "and

here's the rub -

The theories that Physics is conjuring

up to explain this

Start to sound a lot like the magic
and mystery
That we associate with your old
stories!"

"**A**nd where," asks Religion,
"does Life

Fit into your new scheme of things?"

"Well," says Science, "asking questions

of that sort

Has brought us back to the same

path."

"I see," says Religion, "I guess you

must ask yourself:

Is Life itself simply energy particles?

And if so, where does Life begin and

end?

How many energy particles make up

Life?

Those that constitute a body?

Or a brain?

Or a part of a brain?

Or, given the interconnectedness of
all energy particles,
Perhaps the whole universe?"

"Yes," says Science, "I have been
unable to draw a line,
Since the motion of any energy
particle,
Apparently causes motion in every
other.

Whilst I have discovered a lot
about living cells,
And have learnt about the
composition of those,
In terms of chemicals (which consist
of energy particles).
And have been able to predict, and
influence,
And even control growth patterns in
living cells,
I have not been able to capture
The essence of Life –
That which makes cells 'living'.
Nor can I explain how Life,
At least at its higher levels,
Appears capable of making
independent decisions

On what motion should occur."

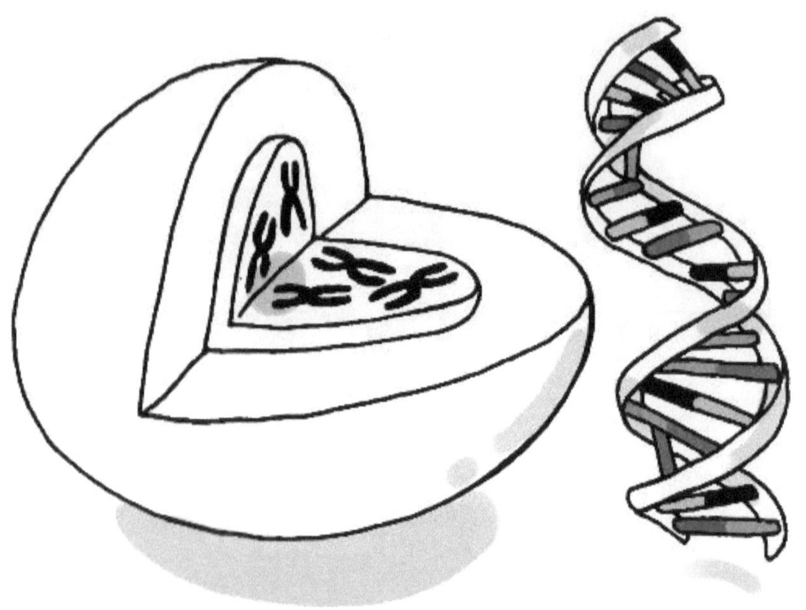

"Your problem," says Religion, "Is
      that Life,

Self evidently,

Can put new order into energy

particles.

Indeed, one can define Life

As that which is capable of,

apparently,

Changing the motion and order of

energy particles

From that motion and order

Pre-ordained by Physics!

And Science is drawn to the same

conclusion

As Religion –

That maybe Life is something
separate from the energy particles?

And capable of directing them in some fashion."

"**Y**ou are right," says Science,
"We can study the motion of
energy particles
But at a certain level, the motion of
energy particles
Does not appear to be compelled
By the motion of other energy
particles.
And here we find Life."

"**W**elcome, once again,
To my world!" says Religion.

"And let us now consider this more carefully together,
And from a different viewpoint.
For Life is not, as Science has sometimes regarded it,
A foreign object of study.
But rather Life is that which does the study.
So the questions:
What is Life?
And, what am I?
Are really the same question.

So let us consider things from the
viewpoint of self.
And ask first the question:
What is a memory?
Does a memory consist of energy
particles?
Before I have a memory I must first
have something to remember.
I see and smell and feel a dog.
A dog (or at least that which I see
and smell and feel)
Is a collection of energy particles.
And my eyes and nose and hands
Are collections of energy particles.
I see the dog because the energy
particles that make up my eyes

React to electromagnetic[4] waves,

known as light,

Emitted (or reflected) by the energy

particles of the dog.

I smell and feel the dog

Because of a chain of energy particle

interactions,

Set off by the energy particles of the

dog,

Create an effect

On the energy particles of my nose

and hands.

And from there the further effect

Of energy particle on energy particle

---

[4] Electromagnetic : caused by an interaction of electric and magnetic forces. Light, radio, x-rays and microwaves are all electromagnetic waves - with different wave lengths.

Eventually reaches wherever it is

That my consciousness resides.

And only then do I see and smell and

feel the dog.

But I can also conjure up in my mind

The sight and smell and feel of a dog

Without the energy particles of a dog

Apparently being physically present.

A memory of a dog
Is the re-experience by my consciousness
Of the sight and smell and feel of a dog
With greater or lesser intensity.

Now, if all that exists
        Is energy particles in space,
Then a memory must also be formed
of energy particles.
Energy particles which I can, by
some process,
Cause to be ordered in that way.
When I think of a dog
I cause energy particles to be
organised
In such a way
That my consciousness can
experience
The sight and smell and feel of a dog
In rather the same way
That my consciousness experiences
The sight and smell and feel of a dog

Which is physically there.

If all is energy particles
And my consciousness'
experience is the same,
What is the difference between
That which is imagined, or thought
of,
And that which is real?

If I can organise energy particles
So that I can see and smell and feel a dog
How do I know
That I do not do that <u>all</u> of the time?
How do I know
That all of the experiences of my consciousness
Were not created by my consciousness?
If I can control some energy particles
Can I not control all?

Does there really need to be an external reality

For me to have an internal reality?

*D*o I make toast?

Or does toast make me?"

*"**I** cannot argue with that logic,"*
says Science,

"For, what do we know?
Of what can we be absolutely sure?
The only thing that you can be sure is
real
Is your own consciousness.
That is sure
Because you are conscious of your
own consciousness.
Of nothing else can you be sure –
Not that I live, or others live
Or anything else exists at all.
Science cannot prove to you that
anything else exists.
Religion cannot prove to you that
anything else exists.

Beyond your own consciousness
All else is faith.

Is there a God?

Is there not a God?

Because the only reality

Is that which your consciousness

decides is real

Either can be true.

Both theism

And atheism

Are a matter of faith.

$\mathcal{A}$nd Science has found its way
back to Religion."

"**B**ut wait," says Religion
"What is a god?"
And answering his own question:
"A god is that which can create
anything and everything.
That could be a description of our
own consciousness."

"**Y**es," agrees Science, "but think
on this:

If our consciousness is responsible for
creating

Anything and everything,

And if we live in a world

Of our own imagination,

And knew it!

Where would be the fun in that?"

"**Q**uite so," says Religion.
"So let there be light
And let there be planets
And let there be others,
And let us be the effect
Of light
And planets
And others.
And pretend that we did not create
them.
Then there would be fun.
Then there would be a game."

"**O**kay," says Science, "but let us
review this further.
We can agree that the one sure truth
Is our own consciousness
And our ability to organise energy
particles
(Or something else, if energy particles
do not really exist)
In order to experience something
Other than nothing.
But how then does anything come
To be <u>real</u> to us
And not just fleeting thought?"
"As I have just said," says Religion,
"By our pretending
That we did not create it,

*Pretending that it is there by some
other cause,
And therefore will continue to be.*

*I*s that what energy particles
really are?
Something that we pretend are
separate from us,
And outside of our creation,
In order to have a life.
In order to have a game."

"There is a way that we can
test this," says Science,
"Something only discovered when we
were re-united.
If we make energy particles appear
By thinking a thought,
Then the existence of those new
energy particles
Should be detectable by the
equipment
Of modern Science
Designed to detect the presence of
energy.
And if we can then make those same
energy particles disappear,
Merely by realising

That we were responsible for their
creation,
Then that equipment will show
That those energy particles have gone
again."

"I see," says Religion, "so what
you are saying is:

When we see energy particles

Truly as our own creation,

And stop pretending that they exist
otherwise,

The energy particles cease to exist.

And a modern monitoring device can
show us

Those energy particles

Both coming and going."

"**Y**es," says Science, "and this has
been done.

And seeing this, perhaps one can
conclude

That it is possible to do this with

Any and all energy particles.

To make them all disappear

By realising that all were our own

creation."

"**B**ut then," says Religion, "Nothing would exist beyond our own consciousness.

Again.

And where would be the fun in that?"

"Yes," says Science, "but perhaps
there are some energy
particles
We could do without?"
"There are," says Religion,
"Pain and fear
Are parts of the game of life.
But why allow past pain and fear
To dominate your present
consciousness.
If we can stop ourselves re-creating
the energy particles
Of the past, which re-create the
traumas
That should be consigned
To history, in our present lives,
Then we can live in the present

And life is much more fun.

*I*f we can stop ourselves re-
creating such energy particles,
Merely by realising that we are responsible
For their creation.
Then we would be clear
Of such unwanted energy particles."

Science and Religion coming together
Make this possible -
Lives unhaunted by past pain and
fear.
And they also make possible a new
horizon,
For with this view of your
consciousness,
This view of your life,
There is a great game to be played.
We can make some assumptions:
Let us assume the existence of others-
For without others there is no game.
And let us grant them equal
beingness
To our own,

And help them achieve the same
freedom.
For if they allow past pain and fear
To dominate their present
consciousness
They will be, to some degree, insane
(Not living in present time)
And where is the fun in that?
For them, or us?
More energy particles we could
really do without.

And then by lifting everyone
To a realisation of the nature
Of their consciousness
And the realisation of what games
Are fun to play.
And which are not.
We can build a new civilization
Where Religion and Science walk
together in harmony
And the games we play
Are fun.

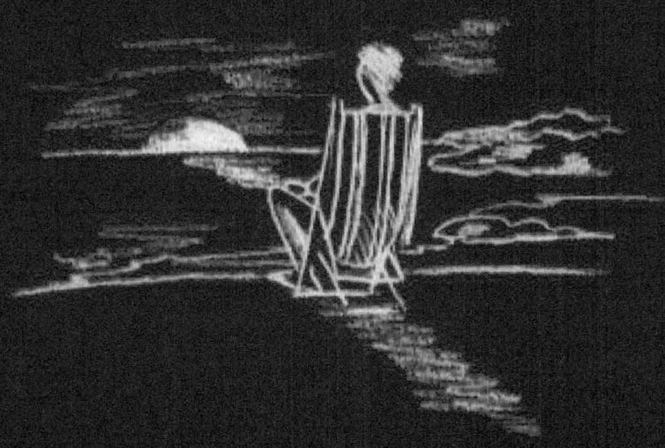

"Beautiful and inspirational."

MAN
V
GOD

P.D. Hodkin

Man v God

Am I looking at the face of God?
Or something God created?
I sit here, on cliff's edge,
Looking out across the tranquil bay,
The sea, the shore, the rocks
Bathed in glorious light.
Shimmering waves, burning sands
and sky,
And the grandeur of the scene
Gives rise to such reflection.

Man is aware of his own existence
Through his own consciousness.
He is aware that he is aware.
And therefore is.
That much is simple and sure.
But how is he aware of others?
Only through their creations.
You create a house;
I notice it and am aware of your existence
To that degree.
You write me a letter;
And in reading it you exist that
much more to me.
You show me your face;
And add to the sum of what you are

To me.
And when everything you have
created
Is removed from my view
You exist still to me
In my memory of all that you have
created
Which I have experienced.
To me you are what you create,
Which I see or otherwise perceive.

And so it is with God?

Nothing exists without a cause,
Is an apparent law of our universe.
But how then did the very first event
Come to be?

God answers that mystery,
The Prime Mover unmoved,
The Creator.

But that God means nothing.
I know that I exist.
I know that I experience things.
If I define "God" as
"That something that causes me to
experience things",
Then God exists.
But that tells me nothing of the
nature of God;
And therein lies the real question.

Should God be worshipped or praised?

Or ignored, or condemned, or just
accepted?
By this definition
God might even be me!

This definition of God does not tell us
Whether God is good, or bad, or
indifferent.
Or whether God is,
Or was,
Even a conscious being –
Such as you and I.
It merely says something kicked
everything off
And we will call that something by
the term "God".

But can we find out what or who God
is?
Perhaps we can.
Just as we learn of the existence of
others
Through our experience of their
creations
Can we learn something of God
Through our experience
Of God's creation?

Now there are those that say
That Man, and the state of the
universe today,
Is the result of a series
Of happy accidents,

Which have occurred since
everything was kicked off.
The happiest accident being life itself,
Which developed and evolved
To bring into existence
Life forms with apparent godlike
power
To create new order and creation in
the universe.
But for our purpose here,
Let us credit that which was
responsible
For the original creation
For having created something
Which could have these happy
accidents.
And, therefore, for good or ill

God is responsible for the state
Of God's creation today.

So what can we learn of whatever
started this universe
(Which we shall call "God")
From what exists in the present?

I, and my fellow humankind,
Are, apparently, the highest
Sentient beings in evidence.
If I am part of God's creation,
What can I learn of God's existence
From considering the nature of me?

Let us start with my current
experience,

As I sit in this high place,
Witnessing a scene of such beauty
And feeling,
Apparently as a direct consequence,
An ecstatic joy
And sense of unlimited freedom.

Why should this be?
What does this tell me
About me?

Does what I see and hear,
And touch and smell,
Have some kind of real external

existence?
Or is it merely
A product of my imagination?

Perhaps this does not matter
For our purpose here.
For what I perceive
Is, in any event, an interpretation
Which is uniquely mine
In all respects.

I look upon apparent objects
And spaces,
Which are both near
And very far away,
Which I assemble,
And attribute qualities to,
Which do not necessarily
Bear any correspondence
To the "true" qualities
Of those objects and spaces

(Whatever that might mean).

At the end of the day,
According to modern understanding,
All physical perception –
Sight, sound, smell and touch –
Is a perception of vibrations.
And that is all.

Whilst it is sometimes said that the
universe
Consists of only energy in space –
Where energy is simply anything
That can cause motion in anything
else.
It seems more accurate to say,
That the universe consists only

Of vibrations in space.
For all forms of energy
Appear to be
Some kind of vibration.

Vibrations of what?
Is the obvious question.
And the answer appears to be
No substance at all.
Or at least when one looks for
substance,
One simply finds other vibrations.

Some vibrations travel across space
In waves
Such as light and sound.
Other vibrations,

At least to an observer,
Appear to be contained
Within a very limited space.
And these vibrations,
Congregated together,
Make up atoms and matter,
And all that appears to be solid,
Or of substance.

And when we see something as blue,
It is not because it is the colour blue,
It is simply that we perceive light
waves
Coming from that direction,
Which have a particular rate of
vibration,
Which we interpret as "blue".

Different colours
Have different rates of vibration.
But we can only perceive
As sight
A fairly narrow band
Of rates of vibration.
Radio waves, microwaves and
x-rays
Are all waves such as light
But with other rates of vibration
Which our eyes
Do not register.

Sound is another wave
That we can detect.
It consists of particles of air
(Or something else)

Hitting our eardrums
And causing another vibration
Which we interpret as sound.
Different sounds have different
Rates of vibration.
And as with sight,
We only register as sound
Rates of vibration
In a fairly narrow range.
Other animals apparently hear
In a different range
To us.

And so it is with all of our
perceptions.
We are bombarded
With different vibrations.

Some of which we are able to detect

As sight,

Or sound,

Or smell,

Or touch.

And some we may perceive,

Or at least experience

The effects of,

In different ways.

And so it is with the scene

I now perceive,

Where my perception

Is simply my interpretation

Of various vibrations

Apparently currently present.

So this then
Is the first thing
I can say about the nature of me –
I am a perceiver
And interpreter
Of vibrations
Apparently emanating
From the physical universe.

But I am not just
A receiver of vibrations,
I can apparently create them
As well.
I am not just a spectator
But also a player.
Not just effect,
But also cause.

I can make my body move
In ways that I intend,
And by such moving
Bring about other motion
In my immediate space.
With my hands
I can snap a twig,
Or throw a rock.
I can speak,
And otherwise make sounds,
Which can be heard
By other life forms
That have a hearing capacity.
(Provided the vibrations
I make
Are within their audio range).

And I can put my body
Into a place
Bathed in certain waves
Having a rate of vibration
Within the spectrum of visible light,
And thereby,
Through reflection of such waves,
Cause my body to be visible
To myself and others
In an array
Of different colours.

And in such manner
I can communicate to,
And cause effect upon,
Objects and other living beings
In my environment.

And I can also create
Chains of motion
To communicate,

Or cause other effects,
Beyond my immediate space.

Indeed, with modern technology,
I can be the cause of motion
On the other side of the planet,
And beyond.

Anything in the physical universe

Can receive vibrations,

And be affected and altered by them.

But only life forms can,

Apparently,

Create entirely new vibrations

And cause new motions to occur.

Life,
At least at its highest levels
(Such as Man),
Appears to be another
Prime Mover unmoved.
Another Creator.
Another God.
Of sorts.

But what I cause
Is often influenced
By the creations of others.
I interact with the rest of existence.
What I receive
Affects what I create,
And what I create
Affects what I receive.

If I only experienced,

Only received,

I would be an object.

If I only caused,

Only created, I would be a God

(As we have defined the term).

But no,

My nature requires both

An inward flow

And an outward flow.

So I appear to sit

Somewhere between object and God;

Sometimes more towards one

Than the other.

But whilst I live

Neither, happily,

At either extreme.

But when I behold this view
I feel like a God.
Exultant.
Powerful.
And at the same time
Calm and serene.
So why should that be
When I did not create it?

And answering this question
May uncover what may be
The most important aspect
Of my nature.
Because the scene before me
Is not inherently glorious.
It is glorious simply

Because I decide it is so.

And what is more,
On another day,
I could sit here,
Before exactly the same scene,
Before the same sight, sounds, smell
and touch,
And lost in some other thought,
Fail to notice it.

I could also lie in bed tonight,
And with eyes closed,
Recreate the scene
In mind's eye
And re-experience
Its joy and glory.

The truth is I am
An editor
And a composer
Drawing material
From both external stimuli
And internal thought.

So that,
Even confronted by such a scene,
The experience of my consciousness
Is actually my own creation.

And when that creation
Is perfect,
Or nearly so,
I feel exulted

And powerful.

And I begin to see the value
Of meditation and of prayer
As occasions
When I take active control
Of the experience of my
consciousness,
And focus my thoughts
On perfect ideals and forms.

Given that the experience of my
consciousness
Is the only experience I ever have,
Or will ever have,
It may be true what they say:
That heaven is not a place,

It is a state of mind.

But let me explore further
What I mean by perfect form.
Why do I consider some things
beautiful?
And some things ugly?
Some things good?
And some things bad?
Some things right?
And some things wrong?

And moreover,
Why do I associate beautiful things
With goodness and rightness,
And ugly things
With badness and wrongness?

And are these things
Just a matter of my taste?
Or is the appreciation of beauty,
Goodness and rightness,
Shared more universally
And intrinsic to the nature of man?

Man certainly likes to put order
Into things.
To steer the random
And chaotic elements of the world
Into forms and patterns
To serve the survival
And continuance of his life form.
And to cooperate with,
And use,

Other life forms
To achieve this order.

So perhaps the answer to what things
Are good or right,
Is that they lead
To better order,
To better survival,
Now, or in the future?

Being honest and fair with others
Does have a survival value for me.
Treating others as I would want them
to treat me
Is a golden rule
And also,
Rationally,

Could lead to better survival for me.

So do I only do things
Which are "good" or "right"
In order to perpetuate
My own life form?
My own current existence?
No, I do not!

That is clearly
Not my nature.
Nor the general nature of man.
For often times
The good or right thing to do
May be directly opposed
To the survival,
Or better survival,

Of the individual.
But done still.

For Man will sacrifice
His own interest,
And sometimes
His own life,
To do,
Or support,
What is good or right.

In fact,
Truth be known,
I tend to measure
The goodness or rightness
Of any action
By the benefit it provides to others.

To family,
Or friends,
Or complete strangers,
Or even animals,
And sometimes to my idea
Of God.
Benefits to self
Are only a small part of that
equation.

Or at least physical benefits.
For let us consider this puzzle
From the viewpoint
Of the experience of our
consciousness.

And here is a curious thing –

There is a very similar
Joy and exultation
When I contemplate being,
Or having been,
Of real value to others,
To the joy and exultation
Evoked by the scene before me.

My current view
Of the universe,
External to me,
Is always seen
Through the prism
Of internal thoughts.
And it seems,
When I contemplate
Current patterns and orders

In the universe,
That there are certain ones
I am pleased to create,
Or pleased to perceive,
And where the experience of my
consciousness
Is an experience of beauty.

For what is "beauty"
But my consideration
Of the order and patterns
Of things in the physical universe,
Which I perceive,
And imagine to exist,
Which I deem good?

Thus I may regard

Sights as beautiful,
Or sounds,
Or actions,
Or states of being.

And in this there are degrees,
I consider some
Orders and patterns
As more beautiful than others.

And in this also
Certain factors
Apparently come into play.
Proportionality is prime among
them.
I deem particular shapes
As preferable to others.

In fact it has long been noted
That there is a golden mean,
Or golden ratio,
Which is very precise,
And found throughout nature,
As well as in Man's designs.
And objects or forms
Having dimensions
Matching the golden ratio
Are universally
Regarded as more perfect
Than those that do not.
And this seems to apply
To everything,
From architecture
To the human face.

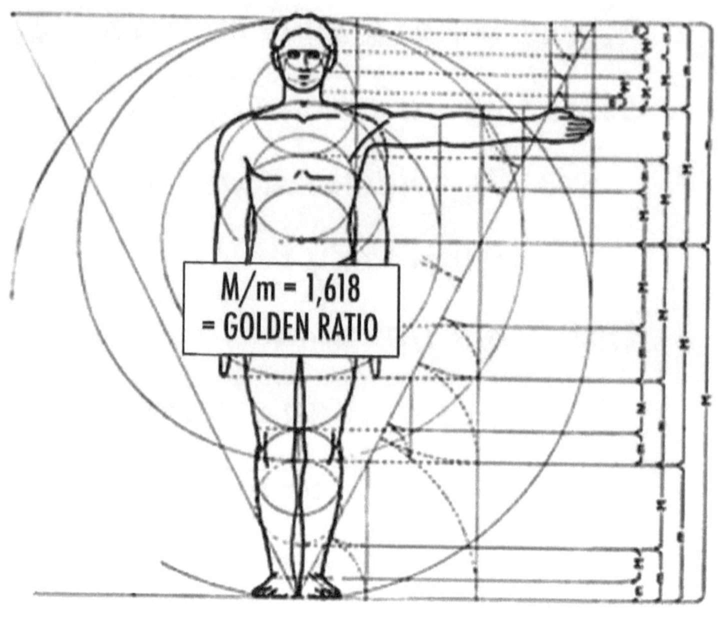

M/m = 1,618
= GOLDEN RATIO

And even a plain rectangle
With sides in the golden ratio,
Of 1 to 1.618,
Will be consistently picked out
As more aesthetically pleasing
Than rectangles
Of other proportions.

Not for nothing then,
Is the golden ratio
Also termed "the divine ratio" -
For it appears to be
God-given,
As we have defined "God".

And, as a cousin to proportion,
We have harmony.

The vibrations
Which we detect as sound
Must have certain rates of vibration
And those rates be in certain ratios,
One to another,
For us to consider them
Pleasing,
And not discordant.

And so it is with vibrations
Which we detect as light and colours.

Out of the random chaos
Of possible vibrations
In the universe
We seek out,
And try to bring about,

Very particular vibrations
And combinations of vibrations.
Not just in sight and sound
But in everything,
Including in all that resonates
From human relations,
In order that the experience of our
consciousness
Is one of beauty.

And whilst it is clear
That there are matters
Of individual taste,
There is a core
Of orders and patterns,
And of how things should be,
Which I instinctively know

Are good and right,
And furthermore,
That I know others know
Are good and right.

If there is such a thing as sin,
It is when I act,
Or cause others to act,
Contrary to what I instinctively
know
Is good and right.
And this is also the basis
Of guilt.

But this knowingness
Of what is good and right and
beautiful

Is what causes me to create things,
And do things,
Which are good and right and
beautiful.

It seems that Man has at his core
A basic goodness –
An innate sense of what a proper,
Or perfect,
Order is.
And whenever we see good
Done in the world
It derives from this.

Selfless acts,
Charity,
Care for and helping others,

Making things better
And more beautiful,
All come from something
Fundamental in our nature
And if we are created this way,
We can thank whatever
Is responsible for creating us.
We can,
Literally,
Thank God,
For all the Man-made good
Done in the world.

If I was created
With a built-in sense
Of what is good and right,
And some means to achieve this,

And whatever was responsible
For my creation
Had planned this,
Then the intention must be
For me,
And others,
To do good and right things.

But if we thank God
For the good,
Then what about the bad?
Selfish acts.
Crime.
War.
Senseless violence.
Do some people see
These things

As good and right and beautiful?
Or do people know
That they are bad, wrong and ugly,
But still they do them?
Either way,
If God has a plan
How does this fit into it?

Let me consider matters
From my own experience.
For I have done things
Which I know to be
Bad, wrong and ugly.
If I can explain my own actions,
Perhaps I can explain
Those of others as well?
What is it about my nature

That caused me to do such things?

Of course there may be times
When I am forced
To do bad things.
Where I am threatened
With pain,
Or other penalty,
If I do not.
Yet whilst I am still in control
Of my own motion,
Even then there is a choice.
But sometimes I feel compelled
To do a thing
I know is bad
By internal,
Rather than external,

Compulsion.

Looking this over,
It seems to me,
That there can be five different
reasons
Why I sometimes do
A bad thing,
A wrong thing,
Or I create something ugly,
Or allow others
To do so.

And these five reasons
Also tell me
Fundamental things
About my nature,

And why I create,
And experience,
As I do.

The first reason
Is the most obvious,
And comes under the heading
Of ignorance,
Or incapability.
I do the wrong thing,
Or create something bad,
Or ugly,
Simply because I do not know
How to do it right.
I paint a poor picture,
I sing out of tune,
I put up a shelf

Which falls down,
I drive into a wall,
I try to help someone in pain
And make it worse.

I just do not know
How to achieve the end
I seek.
I do not know
How to properly use my body,
Or to use the tools,
Or communicate correctly,
To produce the thing
Which is right and good and
beautiful.
So I do it wrong
Or not at all.

The good news is
That this first reason
Can often be addressed
Through education,
Through school,
By learning from the example
Of others.

All positive education
Is about learning about
Orders and patterns
In the universe
Which are good
And right
And beautiful,
And of techniques

Used to bring about
Such orders and patterns.

All we experience
In the physical universe
Educates us.

A good environment
Is a positive educator.
The beauty of the natural world
Is a constant source
Of inspiration.
And man-made beauty
In sights and sounds,
In buildings and towns,
In objects and displays,
And in courtesy and politeness,

And fairness and justice,
And the manner of our relationships
With one another,
All serve as positive examples,
Positive education,
Helping us to achieve the good,
And avoid the bad.

But sometimes a systematic approach
Is required in education.
Sometimes we need to learn
To read and write,
And do sums,
Before we can build bridges,
Or find a way
To save people
From starvation.

One can also, of course,

Have negative education.

One which presents

Something bad or ugly

Whilst pretending it is the opposite.

Or teaches techniques

That produce this result.

And whilst this brings us onto

The second of the reasons –

Since the delivery

Of negative education

Often occurs

In an environment

Characterised by force and duress –

One can view negative education

As simply another contributor
To ignorance and incapability,
Which is the first reason
Why I sometimes do bad things.

As I have already touched upon,
One could view the second reason –
That I do a bad or wrong thing
Because of external compulsion –
As being little,
Or no,
Reason at all.
For even with a gun to my head,
Or a knife at my throat,
Do I not have a choice?

And if my hand was moved

By someone else
Did I do it at all?

If my perceptions and thoughts
Are scrambled or influenced
By the effects of chemicals
And other things in my physical
environment,
Or in my body,
Causing me to lose touch
With the reality of the physical
world,
Then I may not be responsible for my
actions –
If I did not deliberately subject
myself
To chemicals,

And other things,
Having that likely effect.

And what if my actions harmed someone
But saved my family,
Or others,
From starvation or pain?

In an ideal world
We would all live in an environment
Where no one was compelled
To do bad things
Or make such choices.

The third reason
Also bears strongly on all the others.

For this is when I have
An internal compulsion
To do a bad, or wrong, or ugly thing.

I do something,
I know to be wrong,
Which I cannot blame
On lack of education,
Or on duress,
Or other physical factors.
Or I do an action
Which I fail to recognise as wrong,
When ordinarily I would see this.
The former case
May be characterised as being
irresponsible,
The latter

As being out of my mind.

Does the fact
That I sometimes do such things,
In itself,
Invalidate the notion
That I have in innate sense of,
And the natural impulse to do,
Things which are good and right and
beautiful?

Well here is the curious thing
About my nature:
When I have done a bad thing,
And know that I have done a bad
thing,
I just have to find a reason

Why I was not responsible for doing
it!

I,
And I guess mankind in general,
Hate to feel guilty
For doing a bad or wrong or ugly
thing.
And I try to resolve this feeling of
guilt
In one of two ways.
The first is to admit guilt
To myself, and possibly others,
And to make some kind of amends.
Whilst this may be painful,
At least in the short term,
It can resolve the feeling

For good –
And this is why sincere confession,
In whatever context,
Is so valuable,
For myself,
And also others.
For the second way I try
To resolve feelings of guilt,
Is destructive,
And the cause of further harm,
And what is more,
Does not work.
This is where,
Knowing I am guilty,
I pretend that I am not.
And I try to block the memory,
Or alter details in my mind,

To avoid being guilty.

And worse still,
When similar circumstances arise
again,
I repeat the bad or wrong action –
Simply to prove to myself
That I could not help doing it,
And was not responsible.

The first time I did the wrong thing
May have been an accident,
Or due to confusion,
Or misunderstanding on my part.
But it becomes an accident,
Or a confusion,
Or a misunderstanding,

I am determined to prove
I cannot escape from,
And therefore must repeat the
consequences of.

So I repeatedly burn the dinner,
Or lose something,
Or fail to do something on time,
Or even commit a crime,
Pretending to myself
That I cannot stop myself doing it,
And that I am not responsible.

It is,
I admit,
A crazy computation.
That I can avoid feeling guilt

For my original sin
By repeating the sin!

And it does not work.
Because I cannot so easily fool myself
(Although I can sometimes fool
others).
And it is like adding links to a chain
Which I have to carry around.
Or adding to the size of a beast,
I think may eat me,
Which I constantly have to fight
To stop creeping into
The experience of my consciousness.
Sometimes I try to blame others,
And this can get me into
A similarly destructive cycle.

And similarly crazy computations.

As a child
I accidentally stepped on another
child's sandcastle,
And received a thump from that
child.
And that thump not only now
justified
(And I hoped expunged the guilt of)
My treading on his sandcastle
In the first place,
But also justified a further act
Of retribution on my part.
And so a sort of war started between
us,
Which has continued into adulthood,

Often fought in subtle ways.
And all to avoid
Either one of us
Having to admit guilt
For having done something wrong.

As I go through life
I seem to accumulate mental baggage
(For want of a better term)
Of this kind –
Which I use to pretend justifies
Doing a bad or wrong or ugly action,
Rather than doing something
Good, right or beautiful.

There are also times

When the experience of my
consciousness
Is simply overwhelmed
By the perceptions, and information,
it receives.
And apparently switches off,
To some degree.
I go unconscious or faint,
As a result of a sudden impact
Or particularly distressing news.

These times also
Seem to add to my mental baggage.

I banged my head
At a swimming bath
Several years ago,

And a love of water
Changed overnight
To an unpleasant feeling,
A strange, inexplicable nervousness,
When I just feel rain
Upon my face.

As I said earlier,
I need
To both in flow
And out flow
With the physical universe.
And when the vibrations I perceive
and receive
Are understood and processed by me,
And I can respond
In the manner I deem correct –

Like a puzzle solved -
I am happy to let them go.
But, if I cannot do this,
They seem to stay around me,
Like some kind of unfinished business.

It seems that whenever
I have an overwhelming,
Or excess,
Inward flow
(Or sometimes too much outward
flow) -
That is to say,
A situation that I do not feel
That I have been able to resolve
With an appropriate counter flow –
I store it up to resolve later,

Or otherwise just hang onto it,
As more "mental baggage" -
Whilst often trying my best
To ignore it if I can.

And all my "mental baggage",
Sitting just to one side
Of the experience of my
consciousness,
And imposing itself from time to
time,
In response to certain situations,
Apparently outside of my control,
Is not only the third,
But perhaps the most significant
reason
Why I sometimes behave irrationally,

And do not do
The good or right or beautiful thing,
And instead do something
Bad, wrong or ugly.

If my basic nature really is
To do good, right and beautiful
things,
Why do I accumulate
Such mental baggage
Which leads me to do otherwise?
If that is also part of my nature
What does that tell me about God?

But here is something interesting –
I know that I can
Conquer my mental baggage,

And I have seen others do so also.
Sometimes I can eliminate elements
Of it all together –
By finding an appropriate way to
out flow,
Or by admitting guilt for something,
Or otherwise giving up a pretence
That I was not responsible.

At other times I can extract myself
From the effects of my mental
baggage
By simply focusing on things
Which are good and right and
beautiful.

Simply looking at a beautiful scene,

Such as that before me now,
Can temporarily lift me out
Of all my mental baggage.

When my mental baggage
Is not imposing itself upon me,
I feel alive,
I feel in control of my own destiny,
I feel like I am being myself.

And therein seems to lie
The answer to any
Internal compulsion to do
Bad or wrong or ugly things.
The answer is:
To find my true self.

And many before me
Have found this same answer.
To find one's own true self –
To one's own self be true.
And over the centuries
Many techniques have been offered
To achieve just this –
With greater or lesser success.
Prime among these techniques
Is the contemplation of perfect forms,
The inculcation of belief in perfect
forms,
And the teaching of the necessity
To do good and virtuous things
To achieve happiness and salvation.
And if we believe we are created
To do good things,

We can overcome the impulse,
Coming from our mental baggage,
To do otherwise.

So we have space and time to reflect
In a beautiful or ordered
environment,
So we have prayer,
So we have meditation,
So we have the teaching of values,
So we have the teaching of the
existence of God or gods,
And so we have different therapies.

All techniques to lift us out of,
Or permit us to escape,
Our mental baggage –

And create things which are
Good and right and beautiful.

Some may describe this as
Finding or re-finding God,
Others as re-finding one's innate
goodness –
One's innate sense of what is good
and right –
And acting on that innate sense.

It is sometimes said
That we were put here
To work out our own salvation –
To work our way over our mental
baggage
To our own good true self.

But more than this –
If I am to achieve a world
Which is good, and right and
beautiful
I am also going to have to help
Everyone else –
They must also find their true selves.
Or else, they will continue to do
things
Which harm me and others.

To achieve things which are
Good and right and beautiful
I not only have to handle
My own mental baggage –
My own impulses to do otherwise –

But also other people's
As well.

And so it seems that these
First three reasons
Why I sometimes do
A bad thing,
A wrong thing,
Or an ugly thing –
Because of ignorance or incapability,
Or external or internal
compulsion –
May all be conquerable
With the right approach.

And the task of doing this
Is what my life, perhaps,

Should really be all about.

But what of reasons
Four and five?
Because I said I found
Five reasons why I sometimes do
Bad or wrong or ugly things.

Truth be known,
These last two reasons,
Are in a different category
Altogether.

The fourth reason,
I have touched on already -
For in order to do
A good or right or beautiful thing

In one area,

Is sometimes necessary to do

The opposite in another.

So in order to judge

An action properly

I need to introduce the concept of

The "greater good".

Here we have,

To cite an extreme,

The sacrifice of one life

In order to save one hundred.

Or at the other extreme,

The fact that I have

To crush a potato

In order to eat it mashed.

But how do I judge
The "greater good" –
For it is surely a question
On which one can have as many
viewpoints
As there are people
To have viewpoints?

Once again I have to come back
To my, apparent,
Innate ability to recognise
Certain patterns and orders
In the universe
As superior to others –
And my ability to imagine,
And compute,

How certain patterns and orders
today
Can lead to something better
tomorrow.

Even though I am hungry,
I do not eat the seeds.
Instead, I plant them,
And nurture them,
And create a solution
To starvation tomorrow
For myself and others.
And thus I advance the greater good
From the viewpoint
Of the experience of my consciousness
-
Which always includes

Not just my perception
Of the state of things
In the physical universe today,
But also my sense of what
Others are experiencing in their
consciousnesses,
And my thoughts
On how both these things
Will change in the future
As a result of my current actions.

And so I may do a thing,

Which in isolation,

Or seen from a certain viewpoint,

May seem

Bad, or wrong or ugly,

But which in the greater scheme of

things

Is not.

And the opposite

May also be the case.

Something which seems

Good or right or beautiful

May not be in the greater scheme.

A personal pleasure,

Or indulgence,

May be good,

But beyond a certain point

May start to cause harm

To my future self

Or others.

Striking the right balance

Is the real art of living.

And so to the fifth,

And last, reason

I sometimes do a bad or wrong or

ugly thing.

This reason also tells me something

fundamental about my nature.

Imagine the perfect meal –

A meal which combines exquisitely

The flavours you love,

In just the right quantities,

Cooked

And served

Just right.

Now imagine having that meal

One hundred times in a row –

And suddenly a bland,

Cold, toasted sandwich

Becomes quite appealing!

Why?
Because I like variety.
Because I like change.
Because I like a challenge.
Because I like adventure.

Something appears funny to me,
And to others,
At the point of realisation
That an absurd conclusion,
Or premise,
Is actually the correct one.
And this is the secret
Of a good joke.
But absurdity

Is a departure from what is normal,
Or might be expected,
And if one's expectation changes,
Over time,
A conclusion or premise
May cease to be absurd,
And no longer be funny.

Life is about change.
It is also about doing -
When we cease to do, we die.

I am happiest when I believe
I am achieving
Something good or right or beautiful.
Once I have achieved it

I very soon want to move on to
something new,
Or create something even better.
And sometimes I like to start
At the bottom
And work my way up.

So I knock down my house,
In order to build another one.
Or I move to a completely different
environment.

The goal remains the same –
To achieve things
Which are good and right and
beautiful.
But not to get stuck in

The same orders and patterns
Is also important.
And is the fifth reason
Why I sometimes choose
To do something which,
At other times,
I might have regarded
As bad or wrong or ugly.
And why I sometimes welcome
A setback,
A problem,
A challenge,
A new game.

So what then
Do all these observations amount to?

Three things do I know for sure about

me:

I exist.

I have a power of choice.

I have an innate sense
Of what is good, right and beautiful.

Only because of this innate sense
Am I able to make
Good and right and beautiful things
happen,
And stop,
Eventually,

Bad and wrong and ugly things
happening.

I can call whatever force or forces
Were responsible for my creation
"God",
Or not,
As I choose.
But the fact that I have these
Three fundamental qualities
Remains.

Sometimes I have to remind myself
That I have these qualities
To get myself back on the right track.
If I convince myself that I do not
I am lost –

And am likely to do harm
To myself
And others.

The fact that I have
These three qualities –
Was created with these three
qualities –
Is not something I can "prove",
But is self-evident to me
(And I believe is self-evident to
others).

Having faith, and believing also
That I was deliberately created
With these three qualities
Helps me to accept the fact

That I have them,
And brings me more rapidly
Back onto what is sometimes called
The path of righteousness.

It is sometimes hard
(But perhaps not impossible)
To believe
That I have the three qualities
If I do not also believe
That I was created this way
intentionally.
Believing that they are the result
Of entirely accidental,
And random events,
Is not a strong platform
On which the hold to the belief

That I have these qualities at all.

So my God
Did it deliberately.

But these are all
The speculations
Of a cliff top philosopher.

My advice to you,
If you want to do things
Which are good and right and
beautiful
And live in a world
Which is good and right and
beautiful:
Find your true self.

And find your own God.

THE
IMPERFECT
ROAD
P.D.HODKIN

<u>**Chapter one**</u>
<u>**The Imperfect Road**</u>

An imperfect road,

Created by an imperfect man,

With imperfect travelling

companions.

But still a road,

And still,

I believe,

A freedom at its end.

Such is my faith

And the faith of many of my friends.

But it is a faith

Not born out of blind belief,
But out of experience
From actually walking the road.

And how do I know I am on the right
road?
It is because from time to time
I am transported to the road's end.
For a while,
I see and feel what that is like.
A little glimpse of the destination,
Before I return to the point on the
road
I have reached.

And those glimpses become longer,
And more frequent,

The further I travel
Along the road.

And when I am asked:
Why do you walk this road?
Or indeed,
Any road at all?
I tell them about the destination
That I have seen.

The road also gives a meaning
And direction
To my life -
Which often seems absent
From the lives of others.

When I stand on the road,

I know who I am.

I am a consciousness,
Pure and simple.

If I have a location
In the physical universe
No scientist or doctor
Has ever discovered it.

You can take away my arms,
Or my legs,
Or any part of my body
Or brain,
And leave me still.

Which is just as well,

Because if all I was,

Was a sequence

Of atoms and cells -

Just molecules moving around

According to the rules of science,

Then no one would be responsible for

anything.

The thief would say:

"Do not blame me for the crime,

It was the laws of physics".

Thankfully,

Walking the road that I do,

I do not live in that world.

And neither does anyone

Walking the road of any religion.

Because the foundation of any faith

Is that you

Are not an object.

<u>Chapter two</u>
<u>Freedom and Slavery</u>

Great civilisations of the past

Have always depended on a vast

Slave class –

Who supply the toil

So that a few can live well and free.

But the great compromise

Of the modern world

Is that everyone must devote

Some of their toil

For the benefit of others.

And this,

And technology,

And human rights,

And social behaviour,
Means that, whilst we are all this
small part slave,
We are mostly able to live well and
free.
And while there exist places
Where the old imbalances
Still prevail –
Today the greatest threat to personal
freedom
Is the slavery we impose on ourselves.

Ultimately, we live our lives
In our consciousness.
And if our consciousness is full
Of unwanted thoughts,
Of unwanted feelings and impulses

Which appear outside of our control,
We are being an object,
We are being a slave,
And we are not being free.

The only way to improve the quality
of your life
Is to improve the quality of your
thoughts.

Freedom may be defined as:
"The ability to determine one's own
future".
But how could everyone have that?
We do not all want the same things,
And our goals inevitably come into
conflict

To a greater or lesser degree.

So, within the realm of the shared
world,

I must qualify that definition –

And add:

"Within rules that one has knowingly
agreed to".

And, between us, that definition
should suffice.

But there is a realm where
No such qualification is required.

This is the realm of self,

The realm of one's own consciousness.

The realm where one truly resides.

Here one lives,

Whilst one continues to live.
Now.
In two hundred years' time.
In eternity.

In our own universe,
Not shared with others,
True freedom is being in control.

Our lord Jesus said,
The kingdom of God
Is within you.
Our lord Buddha said,
What you think
You become.
The holy prophet Mohammed said,
He who knoweth his own self

Knoweth God.

What I know is:
Your life is what you think it is -
Any other description is for someone
else's benefit.

Chapter three
My House and Garden

I sometimes think

That the world of my consciousness

Is like a house with a garden.

The house being only for me -

Full of my personal thoughts,

And memories,

And imaginings.

And the garden being my

consciousness' view

Of the physical universe,

The so-called real world,

The world I share with others.

I can spend time in the house,
But it can get lonely there –
One can feel like one is nobody and
nowhere.
What I really want,
It seems,
Is to be somebody and somewhere.
To not be nothing.
And that requires others,
To be with others,
And to be in the garden.

When I started
My recent journey
My house was full of all sorts
Of unwanted clutter.
In some rooms I was up to my neck

In dirt,
Barely able to open the door.
The garden I could often
Only see obscured
Through grimy windows.
But I cleaned the house,
And now run through it freely.
And not only can I see the garden
In sharp focus
Through gleaming windows.
But I can run freely out there
As well.

Walking the road
Has given me this.

It has also taught me

To help others
To clean out their houses,
So they too can live,
Most of their time,
In the garden.
And we can have fun together.

And whilst what I describe as my
garden
Is my consciousness's current picture
Of the external world -
In all its aspects -
My picture,
And my garden,
Are not
Exactly the same as yours.

To the degree that our picture is the
same
We may be said to share the same
reality.
When what we see from our points of
view
Is alike
We agree that that is real.

And when our viewpoints differ
There is no consensus as to what is
real.

But if we share the same space long
enough,
And interchange ideas long enough,

We may eventually achieve an
accord,
And see the same things.

But that is not essential,
For us both to enjoy our gardens,
Provided we agree on the basic rules
Of our coexistence.

Rules founded
On what we call
Human rights,
And social
And moral behaviour,
Allow the freedom -
As I have defined it -
To potentially exist

For all.

Chapter four
The Real World

While all that we can ever experience

Is what appears in our consciousness,

And while we believe that there

exists

A universe external to ourselves,

Which we call the real world,

Curiously,

The real world,

So scientists say,

Consists,

Only,

Of energy

In space.

Even matter,
They tell us,
Is made only of energy.

And energy is simply:
Something which can cause motion
In something else.
Which is an odd idea,
If all there is is energy!

And this real world
Of energy and space,
Is perceived by us,
In various ways,
Through our perceptions.
Or so we consider.

By such means it is captured,
And transported
Into our consciousness.

And, by some mechanism,
We can not only experience
The energy and space
Of the physical universe,
But we can also cause motion
To occur there
To a greater or lesser degree.
Although we often think
That our ability to do so,
Directly,
Is limited to the energy and space
Which form our bodies,

And that all other motion
We must cause
By a chain reaction,
Emanating from that location.

There is a flow
Between our consciousness
And the real world.
Both backwards
And forwards.

And wherever
This dual flow exists,
We also consider
Life to exist.

And we are most happy

And serene,
When the flows are moderate
And balanced,
Going back and forth
Like waves on the sea shore.
Neither drowning us,
In a flood,
Nor leaving us parched,
Like in a desert.

<u>Chapter five</u>
<u>Personal Demons</u>

To live is to experience
Energy and space.

But we must always be aware
Of the source of this experience.
Conjuring up energy and space
In our consciousness,
Seemingly derived
From the real world
Or from our known imagination,
Is fine.
But trouble starts
When we allow energy and space

To fester there.

To seemingly have existence

Independent of the real world,

Or knowing imagination.

To impinge on our thoughts

In an uncertain

Or unwelcome way.

For then there is created,

What is sometimes called,

A personal demon.

And the ultimate freedom,

Comes only when we are free

Of personal demons.

Chapter six
The Purpose of Life

The purpose of life,

I have concluded,

Is

To not be nothing.

To achieve this purpose

We have to know

That we have impinged

On the consciousness

Of another.

And moreover,

The thing that we value

More than anything else,

The thing that makes us feel
That we have worth
And are worthwhile,
Is to know that we have created
A welcome experience
For another.

To know that we have impinged
positively
In another's life.

And the answer to feeling depressed
Or low,
Or useless -
As we do from time to time -
Appears to be
Simply this:

Put some order

Or beauty into the world

Which others will enjoy.

Contribute to the happiness

Or well being

Of another person or persons.

Give someone else

A welcome experience,

Or stop them having

An unwelcome one.

Nothing lifts one more than this.

It is the only answer

To feeling fulfilled,

And worthy of existence.

And as this applies
To others too.
Allowing them to give you
A welcome experience,
And to know that they did so,
Will lift them
More than anything else.

It is said that
Salvation comes
By following the example
Of the Saviour.
And that is true.
But for all,
Or any,
To achieve salvation,
We must each be

Both saviour
And saved.

Learn this lesson,
And the lives of everyone
Can be put
On an upwards spiral.

<u>*Chapter seven*</u>
<u>*The Man who Created the Road*</u>

The man

Who mapped the path

I tread

Was not unique

In teaching this lesson.

And whilst others,

Who have taught the same,

Have sometimes been said to be:

A saint,

A prophet,

Or a messenger of God,

He was not.

He was not perfect.

He was a man,
Who lived for adventure,
With an endlessly
Inquisitive mind,
And a capacity for work
Rarely seen.

He saw glimpses
Of the freedom
That all religions seek.

And had a vision
Of getting there,
And of helping everyone else

To get there too.

He started out,
Where we all start,
Standing in a confused place,
Surrounded by the beauty and
pleasures
And the comforts and conveniences
Of the modern world,
But where war and killing
And needless suffering and craziness
Still abound.
And where looking for solutions
Is like looking for tracks
Across a treacherous terrain.

He saw a vast array

Of possible answers and directions,

And trying not to look through

Blinkered eyes,

Carefully examined

The many paths on offer

To discern

Those which really took one forwards

Towards a visionary end

On the distant horizon,

And those which,

Despite the hopes and boasts

Of one vested interest or another,

Did not.

Chapter eight
Mapping the Road

To fully succeed

He had to rout,

Not only his own demons,

But everyone else's too.

Like other great visionaries of the

past.

He sought to map a road.

Like them he was lauded

And admired

By those that found his work helpful.

But also,
Like those whose ideas and thoughts
Similarly challenged established
interests
And authority,
He was misunderstood
And deliberately misrepresented.
Like them he was attacked
He was vilified,
He was mocked and disparaged,
And he had to endure
Demon fuelled protest.

And like them,
He made mistakes,
Took some wrong turns,
And had to retrace his steps.

But, unlike many of them,

He was able to benefit,

From their experiences too.

He tried to map a robust road

That anyone could travel along.

But trying to walk a road

One is simultaneously charting,

Is not an easy thing to do.

And whilst he had lots of help.

It was help, itself,

Full of its own demons.

And people

And instructions

Went awry.

When he left us,
It was hard to say
That he had succeeded.

While I had experienced
Benefits beyond compare,
Some of which
I would even call
Miraculous,
And his solutions had,
Improved,
And saved,
Lives,
Particularly amongst those
Who had reached their lowest ebb,

Still the road

As a whole

Seemed confused

And fragile

And difficult to travel.

But it was also

Not as he intended.

Whilst his work

May have been completed,

The road had not been.

Indeed the truth of the matter was

That the path he had spent

A life time mapping,

The final route that he intended

And instructed -

That road -
Had not yet been built.

<u>Chapter nine</u>
<u>Building the Road</u>

The architect has gone,

Leaving tens of thousands

Of pages of plans.

Sorted,

And read,

In correct order,

The errors

And additions of others,

Fall out.

And the true road

Can now be built.

But it is much easier

To walk a road
Than it is to build one.
Road building is hard work,
And building one perfectly,
Or near perfectly,
Requires a level
Of dedication
And of discipline
That few of us possess.

Fortunately,
Some do.

And the road is built.

Chapter ten
The Road

It is sometimes said

That we see

Only what we want to see,

In any given situation.

A bright and attractive person,

Who I believe has offended

Or crossed me,

In some fashion,

Stands before me,

With a friendly smile.

I do not see their brightness.

I do not see their attractiveness.

I do not see their friendly smile.

I only see the small stain on their shirt.

And so it is with the road.

Those that tried,
And failed,
To build the road,
Or tried,
Unsuccessfully,
To walk the road,
In an earlier construct,
Are sometimes stuck
In that failure.

It often seems that we live in a world
Of cynical gossip,

Where the most prized quality
Is the ability
To make something out of nothing,
And nothing out of something,
On a misinformation
Superhighway.

But walking that path
Has never really benefitted anyone.

It is sometimes said
That there really is
No such thing
As truth:
There are just different degrees
Of lying.

No communication is ever perfect.

If you want me to think well
Of somebody or something,
You emphasise the positive,
And ignore,
Or downplay,
The negative.
Or,
If you want to give the opposite
message,
You do it the other way around.

We all do this,
To some extent,
Particularly if we think
That mentioning faults,

Or redeeming features,
Will lose the point
That we are trying to make.

The trick is to take anything
That anyone says
With a little scepticism,
And to test out any data given
For oneself.
Take as true only those things
You find true for you.
And be prepared to revise
That view.

Such is the attitude required
To really walk
The road.

Not just personal demons,
But having fixed ideas,
Or placing one's complete reliance
In another's opinion,
Act as snares and barriers
On the way out.

The secret to a happy,
Fulfilled,
And vibrant existence
Is to be orderly,
To learn
And apply
Workable solutions
To the challenges of life,
To unburden oneself

Of hidden traps and influences
Which prevent one from flourishing
As one would wish,
And, most importantly,
Be good to others
And allow them
To be good to you.

Do this,
And you will find a better self.
Or perhaps,
Your real self.
Such,
At least,
Is my conclusion.
And such is my journey.

The road to finding
Your true self
Is the road
To walk.

Don't waste your breath

Don't waste your breath

This life is a brief breath in eternity
Rising at dawn and departing at night's call
What fate awaits will be yours to see
You will know the answer in no time at all
The most basic question I can list
Is why does anything at all exist?
Why does not nothing ever be?
But then I realise, I hold the key
Nothing exists unless experienced by me
And knowing that answer will set you free
Those who turn to hate become very small
When like the universe you can be tall

If you want to share your views and comments with the author, he would be happy to hear from you.

He can be contacted on: peter@horizonsnew.com

The Secret of Life... *is available in paperback and on Kindle.*

For more details go to www.horizonsnew.com

9 780957 132429